The Library of Explorers and Exploration

JOHN CABOT

The Ongoing Search for a Westward Passage to Asia

Marian Rengel

the rosen publishing group's
rosen
central

For Mike

Published in 2003 by The Rosen Publishing Group, Inc.
29 East 21st Street, New York, NY 10010

Library of Congress Cataloging-in-Publication Data

Rengel, Marian.
John Cabot : the ongoing search for a westward passage to Asia / Marian Rengel. — 1st ed.
    p. cm. — (The library of explorers and exploration)
Summary: Examines the facts and theories surrounding the voyages taken to North America by the English explorer John Cabot in the late 1490s. Includes bibliographical references and index.
ISBN 0-8239-3626-0 (library binding)
1. Cabot, John, d. 1498?—Juvenile literature. 2. America—Discovery and exploration—English—Juvenile literature. 3. North America—Discovery and exploration—English—Juvenile literature.
4. Explorers—North America—Biography—Juvenile literature.
5. Explorers—Great Britain—Biography—Juvenile literature.
6. Explorers—Italy—Biography—Juvenile literature.
[1. Cabot, John, d. 1498? 2. Explorers.
3. America—Discovery and exploration—English.]
I. Title. II. Series.
E129.C1 R46 2002
970.01'7'092—dc21
                                                                    2002004903

Manufactured in the United States of America

CONTENTS

INTRODUCTION

HISTORY'S FORGOTTEN EXPLORER

There is in this Kingdom a man of the people, Messer. Zoane Caboto by name, of kindly wit and a most expert mariner.
—Letter from Raimondo de Soncino to the duke of Milan, 1497

John Cabot's life story is considered a historical puzzle. An expert navigator from Venice, Italy, Cabot set sail across the unfamiliar waters of the Atlantic Ocean in 1497. His journey would awaken England to the possibilities of the New World, a continent that would later be known as North America. In the summer of that year, Cabot raised the anchor of a small ship in Bristol, England. A little more than a month later, he and his mostly English crew arrived somewhere on the shores of what is now Canada, having crossed the cold waters of the northern Atlantic Ocean.

This statue memorializing John Cabot stands in Newfoundland, Canada. The Italian navigator and explorer attempted to find a direct route to Asia. Although he failed, his descriptions of the plentiful fish in the waters around Newfoundland attracted European fishermen and had a long-lasting impact on the worldwide fishing industry.

This simplified version of Cabot's explorations is also one that historians have painstakingly pieced together from few documents. Because no shipboard logs or diaries have survived to tell us of Cabot's adventure, scholars have little more than secondhand letters to recount the events of his life. No grave marker remains of Cabot, and few, if any, painted portraits of the explorer hang in any museums. His sons exaggerated his achievements, often enhancing them to gain prestige. Sometimes, Cabot's son Sebastian took the credit for his father's prior voyages. Even historians who recorded events within twenty-five years of Cabot's landfall in the New World had to ask the name of the man who sailed from Bristol during the summer of 1497.

More than five centuries have passed since Cabot's Canadian landing. Some historians have relied on his story to bolster Canada's national pride. Others have strongly argued that Cabot, not Christopher Columbus, was the actual explorer responsible for the "discovery" of North America by Europeans. Columbus (1451–1506) may have sailed across the warmer mid-latitudes of the Atlantic Ocean five years earlier than Cabot, but he landed on the islands of the Caribbean. Not until 1498, a year after Cabot's landfall in Canada, did Columbus reach the mainland of South America. Even Amerigo Vespucci, after whom South America was named in 1507, traveled along the southern continent, but he did not set foot on its mainland until 1497 or 1502. Cabot, argue historians convinced of his success, should be recognized for being one of the first of the Renaissance explorers to find the New World.

Most scholars, however, work beyond nationalism and pride to understand the facts of the past and its people. And while regarding Cabot, many question where he and his crew actually landed in Canada. Was it in the frozen lands of Labrador, part of the province of Newfoundland, or the warmer but rockier shores off the coast of Nova Scotia? Did Cabot himself believe that he had found a new land, or, like Columbus, the mainland of Asia?

The answers to many questions about Cabot's life still elude historians. Historical documents and archaeological evidence do not reveal other pertinent information about Cabot's life either, such as exactly when he was born, what he looked like, or how he died.

Scholars are forced to piece facts together about the explorer's history from legal documents and letters that are scattered in the archives of at least three nations—England, Italy, and Spain. They reveal few details about his dealings as a merchant and any business partnerships he had. Historians have learned little about his efforts to gain patronage from England's King Henry VII, who officially supported, but did not fund, Cabot's voyage. The king hoped that the Venetian navigator would find new lands to claim for England.

Finally, if Cabot maintained a ship's log, which historians insist he would have, or if any author documented his voyages, those writings are also either lost or have since perished. Even so, scholars have determined facts that reveal that his nearly forgotten story is one of significance.

Historians since the mid-1800s have worked diligently to discover facts about Cabot's life and accomplishments. This book recounts the latest and most reliable information available about the English explorer, hopefully shedding a much-needed light on his achievements.

1

A RENAISSANCE MAN

That a privilege of citizenship, both internal and external, be made out for John Cabot on account of fifteen years' residence, as usual.
    —State archives of Venice, 1476, translated from the Italian
        by H. P. Biggar in *Precursors of Jacques Cartier: 1497–1534*

John Cabot's name first appears in historical records in 1476, when the senate of Venice, a city-state in northeastern Italy, voted unanimously to make him a citizen.

The document recording the vote, written in Latin, tells historians that Cabot was not born in Venice. To become a citizen, he must have lived there for at least fifteen years. But merely having an address in the city did not grant a person citizenship without first proving his honor. In this case, Cabot needed to have shown the people of Venice that he was a responsible member of the community. To some historians, Venice's requirements for citizenship suggested that Cabot must have been an adult when he requested citizenship,

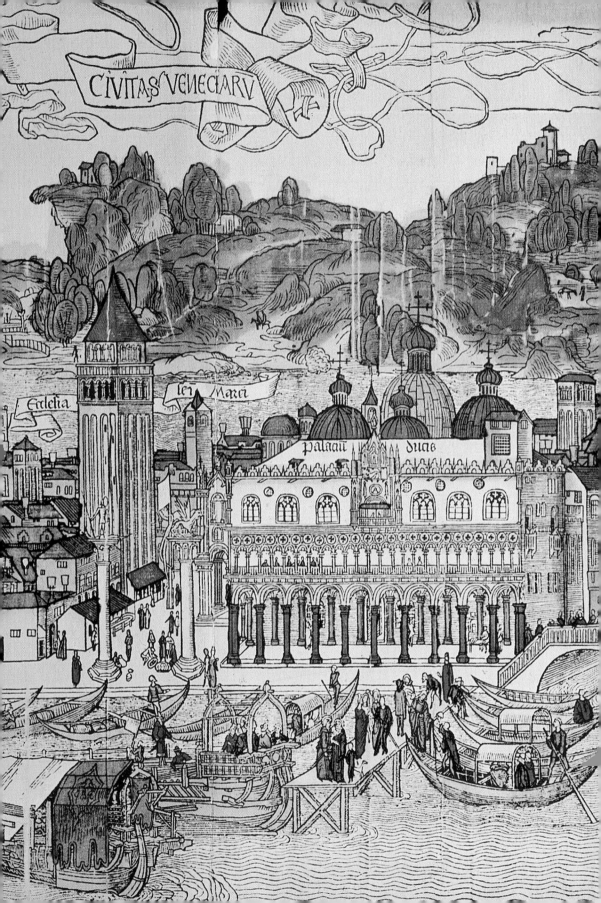

perhaps as young as twenty-eight years of age. (Other scholars have suggested that he could have been as young as sixteen years old, but historians normally calculate Cabot's age based upon the death date of his son Sebastian Cabot, who died in 1557 as a very old man. This has also helped scholars estimate John Cabot's birth year at 1450.)

Cabot's name next appears in Venetian archives on January 13, 1484, as a married man. The record shows that his wife's family transferred a dowry worth seventy-five ducats to him. In return, he gave a bond, or receipt, to "Mathye [Mattea], my beloved wife." The date of these records, however, does not suggest Cabot's actual wedding date, though historians believe he may have been married several years before the money was transferred, as was the tradition.

By 1496, Cabot had fathered three sons with his wife. Their names were Lewis, Sebastian, and Sancio. Although nothing is known of Lewis and Sancio, Sebastian later became famous himself as an explorer of the New World on behalf of England and Spain.

This image of the port city of Venice is from the fifteenth century, when it was the greatest seaport in Europe and the continent's commercial and cultural link with Asia. Venice is still a major seaport and capital of both the province of Venezia and the region of Veneto in northern Italy.

Historians theorize that Cabot could have been born in Genoa, a city-state on the northwestern shore of Italy. In the late 1400s, Genoa was an important seaport. Cabot was "another Genoese," like Christopher Columbus, according to Pedro de Ayala, a representative from Spain, in a letter he wrote to King Ferdinand and Queen Isabella of Spain in 1498. Sebastian Cabot also identified his father as a Genoese, though no record of his birth survives there. Historians believe that, like the lives of other common people, the story of Cabot's birth and youth were not significant enough to have been recorded.

What's in a Name?

Not surprisingly, the man whom history refers to as John Cabot never used the English version of his name. Nor did he use the name dictionaries and encyclopedias refer to as the Italian version of his name, Giovanni Caboto. No original historical documents contain either spelling.

Cabot lived at a time when documents were hand-written and when words, especially names, were spelled in a variety of ways. Some of the many variations of Cabot's name preserved in records written in Latin, Italian, Spanish, and English include Zuan Caboto, Joannes Caboto, Johannes Caboto, and even Zuam Talbot.

This signed letter from Cabot's son Sebastian dates from about 1533. Sebastian was an accomplished mapmaker and navigator in his own right. In 1508, with King Henry VII's support, he set out to explore lands of the New World for England. He also explored the coast of North America and spent four years sailing off the east coast of South America for Spain.

Conflicting Evidence

While most historians accept the statements of Pedro de Ayala and Sebastian Cabot, who both claimed that John Cabot's birthplace was Genoa, two alternative possibilities of his origin have yet to be disproved. Records in Valencia, Spain, contain a letter written by King Ferdinand in 1492 that identifies "Johan Caboto Montecalunya, the Venetian." This mariner proposed building a major port on the beach of

Valencia. Historians have not been able to find a meaning for the word "Montecalunya," but some suggest that it has a Spanish origin, particularly a dialect from Catalonia, a region of Spain north of Valencia, which suggests that Cabot may have been born in Spain.

In one other case, the English historian Rawdon Brown wrote on a copy of his 1838 article as it was recounted in the James A. Williamson book, *The Cabot Voyages and Bristol Discovery Under Henry VII*, that he had found new evidence about Cabot's origin. Brown claimed he had found proof that the man who established England's claim to the newly discovered continent was English by birth. Many historians have argued recently that Brown's claim was an attempt at nationalism. They say Brown was trying to support with hindsight England's claim to the land and its riches. The documents to which Brown referred have never been found, despite intense searches.

Merchant of Venice

Cabot was a Venetian merchant, according to a letter written in December 1497 by Raimondo de Soncino to the duke of Milan, telling him of Cabot's recent voyage. Apparently, de Soncino knew Cabot well and talked with him about his life. Cabot was an expert mariner and a skilled navigator, according to de Soncino, and would have been well acquainted with the art of sailing the ocean. At the time Cabot learned to sail, he was familiar with the highly lucrative North African spice trade.

In Italy, the Renaissance, or rebirth of art and learning, had reached the heights of artistic and scientific influence in the fifteenth century. This time of intense cultural activity served as a transition period between the Middle Ages (fifth through thirteenth centuries) and the more modern, scientific era. Navigation, exploration, and expanding European trade routes were other primary characteristics of this dynamic period, and Cabot, along with other explorers of the day, was a part of that intense journey of expansion and discovery.

De Soncino wrote that Cabot had told him of previous trips to Mecca, an ancient city on the Arabian Peninsula. There Cabot might have learned of the riches traders brought overland by caravan from Eastern countries such as Cathay (China) and Cipango (Japan). In the markets of that city, Cabot might have learned of the months it took men and animals to haul the spices on foot and caravan through the deserts of distant lands. He also probably heard stories of other peoples or great societies. It was in Mecca that Cabot most likely began his dream of finding an ocean route—rather than one over land—to those Asian riches.

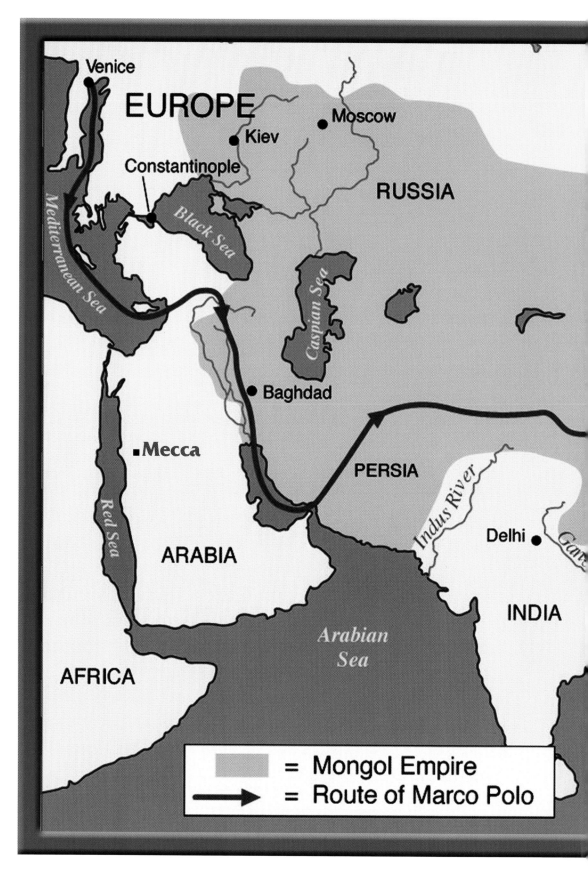

Venice

EUROPE

Moscow

Kiev

Constantinople

Black Sea

RUSSIA

Mediterranean Sea

Caspian Sea

Baghdad

Mecca

PERSIA

Indus River

Delhi

Gan

Red Sea

ARABIA

INDIA

Arabian
Sea

AFRICA

Arabian Sea

= Mongol Empire

→ = Route of Marco Polo

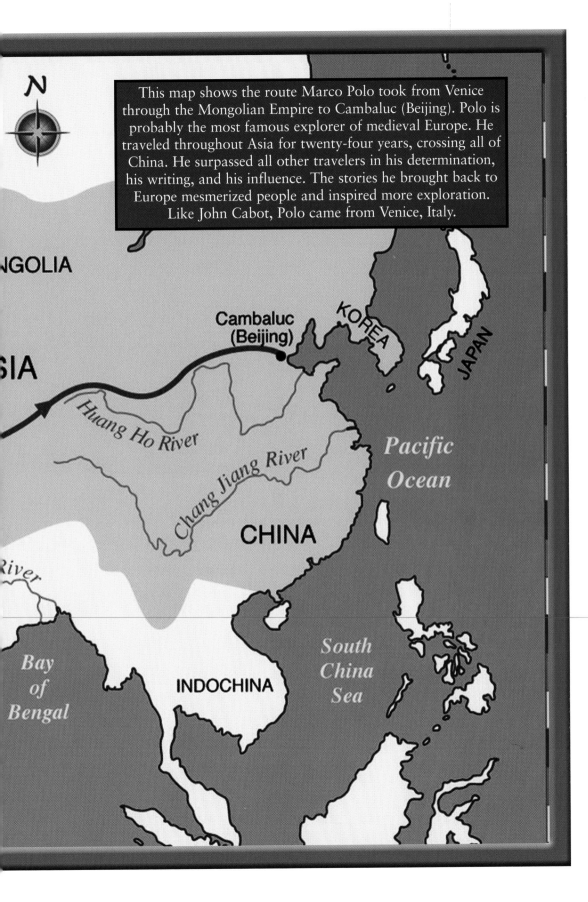

This map shows the route Marco Polo took from Venice through the Mongolian Empire to Cambaluc (Beijing). Polo is probably the most famous explorer of medieval Europe. He traveled throughout Asia for twenty-four years, crossing all of China. He surpassed all other travelers in his determination, his writing, and his influence. The stories he brought back to Europe mesmerized people and inspired more exploration. Like John Cabot, Polo came from Venice, Italy.

Cabot probably spoke with friends about locating Cipango, the ancient land of the Far East made famous by Marco Polo (1254–1324), another Venetian traveler. Cabot longed to reach Asia and its wondrous riches, and his trade missions to Mecca ignited and fed his dream.

Cabot imagined that if caravans carried riches for months and years across the great land mass of Asia, then ships sailing westward around Earth could reach those same lands of wealth in much less time. Cabot's dream was based upon the resurgence of knowledge in Europe from ancient cartographers such as Claudius Ptolemy, who greatly underestimated the size of Earth when he created the first map of the world in his groundbreaking book, *Geography*. While most people at the time understood that Earth was round, navigators also underestimated the total size of Earth. Cabot, like his contemporary Columbus, did not believe the world was large enough to hold two additional continents and two vast oceans.

Another letter offers evidence of Cabot's desire to sail west to Asia. In 1498, the same year that Vasco da Gama navigated a sea route to India for Portugal, de Ayala, in a letter to the Spanish

Goods flowing through Egypt from the east would have arrived mostly on the well-traveled sea routes of the Indian Ocean and the Red Sea. The idea behind new European sea routes was not to replace overland routes from China but to bypass Italian and Muslim traders in the Mediterranean region.

monarchs, confirmed that Cabot had been to Lisbon, Portugal, and Seville, Spain, "seeking persons to aid him in [his] discovery [of foreign trade routes]."

These discussions are the only evidence of Cabot's early career as a navigator, yet historians argue that only the merchants of Italian port cities such as Venice or Genoa, and not Bristol, England, could have had enough knowledge of navigation to attempt a voyage across the Atlantic in the 1400s. Historians suggest that King Henry VII hired Cabot because of his specific abilities as a navigator, valuable skills that he most likely would have gained only in Italy.

While Cabot would have needed to prove himself to England's king, the proof of Cabot's know-how is in the investment provided by the experienced businessmen of Bristol. Cabot's dream of reaching Japan matched their desires of finding riches in Asia. The meeting of those goals—navigational success, new trade routes, and the resulting profits, as well as England's desire to expand its territory—resulted in one of history's most important voyages.

2

SECRETS OF THE NORTH ATLANTIC

It is considered certain that the cape of the said land was found and discovered in the past by the men from Bristol.
—John Day, 1497, in a letter to Christopher Columbus,
translated by L. A. Vigneras

Many twentieth-century historians argue that John Cabot was not the first European navigator to visit the shores of Canada. From the Norsemen (Vikings) of Scandinavia in the tenth and eleventh centuries to the merchant sailors of Bristol, England, in the 1480s, Europeans appear to have regularly crossed the Atlantic Ocean.

In fact, Cabot's command of the *Matthew* in 1497, as we shall see, marked an end to the haphazard and chance landings on the North American continent. It led to the beginning of well informed, planned, and successful expeditions and explorations for the kingdom of England.

An eighth-century Viking trading ship leaves on an expedition from Norway in this illustration. The Vikings were seafaring warriors who raided and colonized wide areas of Europe from the ninth to the eleventh centuries, and whose disruptive influence affected European history. In about AD 985, Bjarni Herjolfsson, a Norse settler in Greenland, sighted a continent west of Greenland, but he did not go ashore. About fifteen years later, Leif Eriksson, son of Erik the Red, explored the new continent. Over the next ten years, the Vikings made a number of voyages from Greenland to North America, which the Norsemen called Vinland.

Norse Settlers

The evidence of Norse visits to the shores of North America stems from archaeological research conducted in Greenland and from legends and documents that have survived in Iceland and Norway. Erik the Red, after being expelled from his native Norway and then from Iceland, traveled in AD 986 with fourteen ships filled with family members and colonists to settle in western Greenland.

Research by archaeologist Kirsten Seaver suggests that he and his companions frequently traveled to the coast of Labrador, a province of Newfoundland, which lies more than 500 miles west of Greenland. Other studies indicate that Norse sailors may have traveled as far south as Nova Scotia and the Saint Lawrence River. Further research, primarily by Canadian archaeologists, shows that Erik the Red's son established a permanent Norse presence in what is now L'Anse aux Meadows on the northern part of the island of Newfoundland.

A closer examination of Scandinavian documents also suggests that for centuries Norse settlers in Greenland made seasonal journeys along the North American coast, harvesting foods from its ocean and shore. Historians think that the Norse descendants inhabited

Greenland in the early 1400s and may have been visited frequently by fishermen from Iceland, Ireland, and England, who then would have learned of the fishing grounds along the Canadian coast.

Bristol and North America

Research into the merchant trade of England has led to a significant understanding of the trading business that built the English port city of Bristol. For example, in 1956 a letter was discovered in the Spanish archives in Simancas, Spain. It was written by Bristol merchant John Day late in 1497, and it told of ocean voyages in the 1480s. "It is considered certain that the cape of the said land [upon which Cabot landed on June 24, 1497] was found and discovered in the past by the men from Bristol." This statement, by a man who had firsthand knowledge of Bristol's business, suggested that merchants had financed annual expeditions of fishing fleets to the unnamed land across the Atlantic Ocean since late in the fifteenth century. Additional evidence suggests that the Bristol merchants, as long as they could have afforded to, also had sent expeditions to the west.

Historians and archaeologists have worked to uncover evidence of any connection between Europe and North America. In many instances, they have provided evidence of almost continuous seafaring between the two continents. Scholars have gathered so much evidence, in fact, that many have developed theories about how Cabot, a navigator who knew well the waters of the Mediterranean Sea and the Atlantic Ocean along Europe's western shores, "discovered" a new continent.

But North America was not lost. Scholars increasingly point out that some Europeans already knew that the land existed. And although mariners did not know the extent of the continent, neither north nor south nor east nor west, they apparently believed that the distant shore was not Asia, contrary to the beliefs of many more experienced navigators.

The Westward Route

For Cabot, the late fifteenth century marked a perfect moment to combine his personal business interests with the political and expansionary goals of England's king, Henry VII. As historical documents suggested, Henry wanted to control those same riches and, in the event that a continent stood between England and Asia, to gain dominion over whatever lands could officially be made known to him.

This map of details of the New World was made by German cartographer and navigator Martin Behaim in 1520. In 1492, Behaim made the first known terrestrial globe. Historians believe that Behaim also introduced brass astrolabes to replace wooden models.

CANCRI TROPICVS

INSVLE CANIBALOR
SIVE ANTIGLIE

Anthong

Alba

Salis

Vifi

Anranuca

Farium

Samona

Laonigo milinga

Deferana

Margalais

Phillippi

Domana

Aloen. Porcellana et Campella. Infula 440 milliaris Longitudo Imperia per Christofer. regis Castiliae capitaneū anno domini 1492

Insula portugalensse Hexici insentis Anno dm 147

NVS OCCIDENTALIS

Lasgaias
Canibales

La ponta
de la galeis

330 P se arena

340

350

TERRA
PARIAS

Rio de Paria

CANIBALOR TERRA

Sera S. Maria

for osa moso

NOVA

Qui hanc in habitard Antropop gi sunt Apua eos Brasileu ch cham Cassia fistula ca silliestiri joi et nara be

baria ge suasum

Marie

S. Michael

Hic margarit rum & di copia

AMERICA VEL
BRASILIA SIVE
PAPAGALLI TERRA

R de pereia

Rio grāt

Porto real

Hieronimi

Monte fregosp
Abaña omnisclar

R de oio
Re de mese

CAPRIC

MASI

Hic regin

In the letters patent, or public letters, of March 5, 1496, King Henry VII gave "full and free authority, faculty, and power to sail to all parts, regions, and coasts of the eastern, western, and northern sea, under [England's] banners, flags, and ensigns." This authority from England's king made Cabot's voyage of exploration more important than any of its prior voyages.

Shortly after Columbus's historic journey across the Atlantic Ocean in 1492, with the support of the Spanish royalty, sending exploratory missions across the ocean became a major goal of most western European countries. England, not yet the powerful naval force it would become by the mid-1500s, entered the contest as well, but details of the kingdom's efforts were so slight that records do not identify exactly when Cabot arrived in Bristol.

3

DREAMS REVEALED

We have been informed by Johan Caboto Montecalunya, the Venetian, that he arrived at this city two years ago and during this time he has considered whether on the beach of this city a port could be constructed.
—Letter written by Spain's King Ferdinand to the governor-general of Valencia, Spain, 1492

John Cabot was "a most expert mariner," according to Raimondo de Soncino, and very knowledgeable about the latest instruments for guiding ships across ocean waters. To gain such knowledge, he would have needed many years of experience crossing the Mediterranean Sea and sailing to ports in Italy, Spain, and the Middle East. But because historians know so little about Cabot's early career as a navigator, they have relied upon facts about other seafaring men to arrive at educated theories about his sailing experience.

As a young man, Cabot likely served in many positions aboard ship, apprenticing to captains, studying nautical instruments, and learning about life at sea. A trip from Venice to Mecca on the Arabian Peninsula, for instance, would have involved crossing the Mediterranean Sea

to Alexandria, Egypt, and then setting out across land in a southward direction.

And if he is the same Johan Caboto Montecalunya who in 1492 proposed building a port in Valencia, then he would have learned about harbors, the depth of water needed to bring in trading vessels of the era, and the materials needed to establish a stable ocean floor.

Scientific Knowledge

If Cabot was born in 1450, he would have been forty-six years of age when King Henry VII approved his Atlantic Ocean crossing. By 1496, Cabot could easily have gained more than thirty years of experience at sea. He would have been well acquainted with the astrolabe and the cross-staff, and perhaps even the quadrant, all devices for determining latitude, or positions north and south. He would have known how to use a magnetic compass for finding direction. Yet Cabot, like his colleagues, would have had great difficulty measuring longitude, or positions east and west, for that skill eluded navigators until the development of reliable marine clocks in the 1700s.

Cabot (standing) presides over a conference of cosmographers. Cabot thought that the world was bigger than Columbus had claimed and that it would be time-consuming to sail straight from Spain to Asia. Cabot devised a simple plan to sail from a northern latitude where the voyage would be much shorter. Sailing west, he could reach land fairly quickly and coast southward until he found Japan. His scheme might have worked were it not for the North American landmass.

Most scholars suggest that knowledge of Earth's spherical shape was understood among the people of Europe in the 1400s. While that view was shared by the masses, many historians also believe that the educated elite had for centuries thought that the world was round. Columbus, Vespucci, Magellan, and other European explorers had the scientific knowledge and the skills to understand that Earth is round.

An astrolabe is an instrument used to measure the altitude of stars and planets. From this the navigator is able to figure a ship's latitude, or its distance north or south of the equator. By the mid-fifteenth century, astrolabes were adopted by mariners and used in navigation. The astrolabe above is from 1569.

These same navigators, however, lacked a true understanding of Earth's size, or circumference. Cabot, like his peers, believed that a short journey of less than a month, not more than two months, lay ahead of them when they set sail in a westerly direction to Asia. They did not understand or appreciate that the world was large enough to contain two additional continents and two huge oceans. Europeans did not realize until

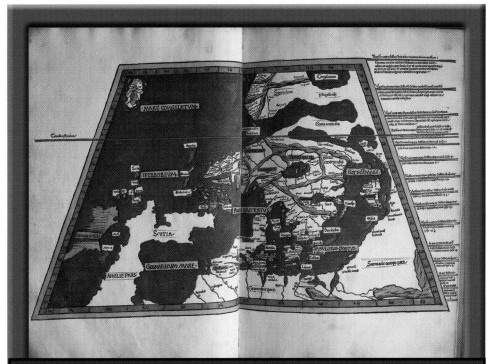

This map of northern Europe was made in 1482, using calculations made by the second-century astonomer Ptolemy, who greatly underestimated the size of Earth when he created his first map of the world.

the early sixteenth century that the great Eastern Ocean Marco Polo had written of in his memoirs in 1298 was not the same ocean that lapped upon the shores of Europe.

A Dream of Discovery

While Cabot's journey to Mecca had taught him about the spices, gems, clothes, and woods that came in abundance from Asia, he shared Columbus's dream of finding a sea route to its shores. He also believed that traveling in the opposite direction—sailing west—would bring him more swiftly to those riches.

33

In March 1493, when Columbus was welcomed to the harbor at Palos, Spain, from his first journey across the Atlantic Ocean, Cabot may have been there. If Johan Caboto Montecalunya is the same Cabot who sailed to the new lands in 1497, then he was in Valencia, on the Mediterranean coast, when Columbus returned. Cabot could have been among the crowds that welcomed the Genoese hero in cities across Spain. It is possible that Cabot met Columbus and doubted his story about reaching Asian shores.

Once he had heard of Columbus's failure to reach Asia in warmer waters, Cabot, some historians argue, probably concluded that a journey across the Atlantic Ocean's cold northern latitudes would be more effective. Because the earth's lines of longitude are much closer together in the north because of the curvature of the planet, he concluded, the journey would be swifter. Cabot believed he could sail westward in far fewer days than the ten weeks Columbus had required. He may have thought he could reach the Asian mainland in record time before sailing in a southerly direction along the coast until he found the great societies of Marco Polo's stories.

Even if Montecalunya is not the same man who made that North Atlantic journey, historians suggest that England's Cabot would have also been well acquainted with Columbus's struggle in the 1480s to find a government

This picture illustrates Columbus leaving on his first voyage from the port of Palos in southern Spain on August 3, 1492. He was bound for the Indies across the Atlantic Ocean. It was on this trip that he "discovered" America.

to support his quest. Cabot, a Genoese navigator like Columbus, could easily have learned of any efforts to cross the Atlantic in the southern latitudes. Cabot, sharing that dream, could have formed his own plan, influenced by Columbus's reasoning, to reach the same destination by a shorter, northern route.

Cabot apparently also sought financial support from the leaders of Spain and Portugal, just as Columbus did. Cabot, however, found little success in those countries. Spain had already agreed to pay for Columbus's journeys, supporting a second voyage of seventeen ships and 1,500 men that would not return until 1496. Portugal had little interest in repeating Spain's success and instead pursued its own goal of exploring the western coast of Africa. Portugal had a critical success when Vasco da Gama, a Portuguese navigator, became the first European explorer to round the Cape of Good Hope on his journey to India from 1497 to 1498. That said, England remained the next best seafaring kingdom after Portugal and Spain that Cabot could approach with his dream of westward exploration.

Bristol, England

The ports of Europe in the 1400s were busy places, with people from around the known world meeting, talking, and sharing information. Bristol merchants traveled to Portugal, Spain, and Italy, just as merchants from Venice traveled to Spain, Portugal, and England. Historical records of the day-to-day activities of trading centers that lined the Mediterranean Sea and Europe's coast suggest that Cabot most likely met merchants from many distant cities, including Bristol, as he traveled to find financial support for his voyage.

It is also possible that merchants from Bristol traveled to foreign ports seeking a talented navigator willing to take on such an adventure on England's behalf. Or Cabot easily could have made contact with such

This map of sixteenth-century Bristol (also known as Brightstowe, Brygestowe, or Bristowe—"the place of assembly by the bridge") shows the city at the convergence of the River Avon and the River Frome. Bristol has been a center of trade since its harbor was improved in 1247 by diverting the River Frome to the west and building a stone bridge where the two rivers join. By the sixteenth century, Bristol was a major port, manufacturing town, and distribution center for both overseas and inland trade.

merchants in Venice, Seville, or Lisbon and reached a business agreement that took him to the royal court of England.

Cabot most likely moved with his family to England in the mid-1490s, a time when he, a talented Venetian merchant, might have seen opportunities for exploration. By helping England achieve its mercantile goals and enabling its king to enter the competition to reach Asia by sea, Cabot could also fulfill his own ambitions.

St. John's Church in Bristol, England, was the gateway to the city in Cabot's time. Cabot, like other Renaissance explorers such as Christopher Columbus and Amerigo Vespucci, probably made a last stop at church before departing on an ocean voyage.

By 1495, Cabot, his wife, and their three sons had become residents of Bristol, where they rented a small house on Saint Nicholas Street. Bristol was a lively, thriving city of cobblestone streets and row houses located at the junction of the River Avon and the River Frome, just about eight miles from where the Avon empties into the Bristol Channel. The Avon was a treacherous waterway: Not only was it difficult to navigate, but its tidal flow was extremely forceful. Still, Bristol's location was in a prime position if one were thinking of sailing toward the channel and farther into the Atlantic Ocean in a westerly direction, as Cabot had intended.

Once there, Cabot met merchants who would later help him finance his voyage. He became friendly with two of Bristol's most successful businessmen, Robert Thorne and Hugh Elyot. Both men provided details about the city's trading history, its interests, and recent voyages. In turn, Cabot certainly shared his desires of searching for unknown lands in the name of England.

By the end of the fifteenth century, Bristol—then a city of 10,000 people—had become England's most prosperous port, importing and exporting taxable goods such as cloth, wine, and dyes to and from Spain, Portugal, and Ireland, and wool and salt to Iceland. But trade in Iceland had slowed, and its fishing industry was facing an economic slump. (English sailors had conflicting trade agreements with Icelanders for years, the results of which were finally beginning to affect profits.) Because of this, England was in search of a new base for lucrative fishing operations that would result in increased profits. To solve this problem, Bristol had seen many ships leave its docks in search of new lands and untouched fishing grounds.

Brasil and the Island of the Seven Cities

As it happened, the mariners and ship captains who worked the port in Bristol believed in the existence of distant, but unknown, lands in the Atlantic Ocean. Sailors, who often spoke about what they had heard or seen on their voyages, shared stories about an island called Brasil (also known as Hy-Brasil) that was said to lie off the coast of Ireland. Other legends claimed that there was another island, too, only this one contained fabulous riches and was known as the Island of the Seven Cities.

English ships had been searching for undiscovered territory in the Atlantic since 1480. Some historians believe that British sailors explored areas as far north as present-day Canada. A few sailors claimed they had spotted the sight of land to the south and west of Greenland in waters that were regularly traveled by English boats.

This news excited Cabot, who knew he could use the evidence of distant, unknown lands to convince King Henry VII to support an official voyage of exploration. To Cabot, these islands of riches sounded like the islands lying off the coast of Asia—the same islands that Columbus mistakenly believed he had found in 1492.

Cabot sought financial support from the city's merchants and political support from King Henry VII for his official journey. In the highly competitive seaport of Bristol, Cabot sought the means to fulfill his long-held dream of sailing west in the Atlantic's icy waters to the mysterious lands of Asia.

4

THE DARK AND PERILOUS SEA

We have also granted to them and to any of them, and to their heirs and deputies of them and any one of them, and have given licence to set up our aforesaid banners and ensigns in any town, city, castle, island or mainland whatsoever, newly found by them.
—Official letter from England's King Henry VII to Cabot, 1496

Besides his dreams, Cabot took with him to Bristol his skills as a savvy navigator, ship's pilot, and cartographer. His plan was to use his talents to find, record, and claim new lands for England.

Cabot's hope was to sail to Asia, not around the long, unknown coast of Africa, but by the shorter route, a westward journey across the Atlantic Ocean. He and other Italian mariners of the day, most notably Columbus, believed a direct route lay to the west of Europe. If the world was round, they reasoned, the journey was possible.

King Henry VII moved England toward an absolute monarchy, which was based on his belief in the divine right of kings to rule without having to answer to nobles, the church, or members of Parliament. He was an able administrator, but he was frugal. When he came to the throne, the Crown was heavily in debt, but when he died, he left a bulging treasury. It is not surprising that the king also supported, but did not finance, Cabot's journey in 1497.

Anno H·o·5·zq oktobe· imago henzirh vii· tzaurcgz zrgie Walterssim
ozdinata p herman zmck Po zrgie gliberum

Fueled by the stories he heard in England, his experiences while trading in the Middle East and Egypt, and his interest in Marco Polo, who had told the world of the great riches of Asia 200 years earlier, Cabot was about to fulfill his destiny.

Seeking Patronage

Somehow, and historians argue over his method, Cabot convinced King Henry VII, who was fond of riches, to give public support to his expedition. Cabot traveled to London and the king's court in late 1495 or early 1496 to begin to plead his case with his advisers and then, eventually, with the king himself.

History provides no evidence of how Henry VII came to sign the charter, or letters patent, for Cabot's voyage. Through his own words or words drafted for him, Henry granted to the "well-beloved John Cabot, citizen of Venice" permission to sail west from England's shores, "under [England's] banners flags and ensigns," seeking "islands, countries, regions or provinces . . . which before this time were unknown to all Christians."

Scholars of the late twentieth and early twenty-first centuries suggest that Cabot became a public symbol for Henry VII's efforts to expand England's kingdom. Now that Spain was gaining a foothold on the lands of the New World, England, then a country of great poverty,

Henry VII gave his official royal support for Cabot's expedition in a public document. As an agent of England, Cabot was empowered to investigate, claim, and possess lands "which before this time were unknown to all Christians," which meant he could not intrude on Spanish and Portuguese discoveries. Henry VII would receive one-fifth of the value of merchandise brought back to Bristol, although the king had not invested English money in Cabot's journey.

was pressured to discover new lands and trade routes of its own. (The Black Plague and a long civil war had left the kingdom politically divided and virtually bankrupt.) If Cabot was correct in his belief about the mysterious islands lying off the coast of Asia, then England could single-handedly control the elusive and profitable spice trade, saving England from financial ruin. Surely, Cabot probably argued, the English could still beat the Portuguese and Spaniards to

China and Japan, especially since by his reasoning Asia was physically closer to England than either of those kingdoms. The king, having refused official support to Columbus years earlier, did not wish to make a similar mistake this time. In this very knowledgeable Venetian merchant, Henry VII likely saw the opportunity to successfully enter a kingdom-building venture.

The Treaty of Tordesillas

If King Henry VII supported Cabot's decision to sail west in search of a new sea route to Asia's wealth, however, he risked the possibility of conflict with both Portugal and Spain, since both kingdoms had staked claims to lands in the Atlantic Ocean. Together, both had signed the Treaty of Tordesillas in 1494, which divided the lands in the Atlantic Ocean by an imaginary line.

The terms of this treaty, which divided the area vertically from the North Pole to the South Pole 370 leagues (approximately 1,100 miles) west of the Cape Verde Islands, gave Spain the land west of the line and Portugal the land east of it. But King Henry VII had not been invited to sign the treaty and was not legally bound by it. Therefore, he decided that undiscovered lands in the same latitude as England were available for exploration by any navigator sailing under the English flag.

Charting His Course

Cabot finally received the king's permission to sail on March 5, 1496. His plan for reaching Asia was to exploit Bristol's strongest winds while sailing down the Avon to the mouth of the Bristol Channel and into the sea. Next, he planned to travel across a short section of the Atlantic Ocean to southern Ireland before heading west from the shores north of Dursey Head.

While Cabot had gained his experience sailing around the Mediterranean Sea, Bristol's merchants knew very well the fishing waters off the coast of Iceland, more than 800 miles north-northwest of their English port. They also understood the seasonal winds of the waters around England. Cabot, applying his expertise to this knowledge, was determined to catch the easterly winds of late May to power his journey. For some reason, however, Cabot's memorable voyage of 1497 set out fourteen months after the king had authorized it.

A First, Unsuccessful Voyage

For the first 450 years after John Cabot was known to have reached the North American continent, historians, some who lived when Cabot lived, recorded only the story of his 1497 voyage. But in 1956, a scholar named

47

Although his first voyage failed to reach Japan, Cabot remained undeterred. In the months after returning to England, where his trip was considered successful, he made more careful arrangements for his second attempt to find a new sea route to Asia's wealth.

L. A. Vigneras, studying in Spain's national archives in Simancas, uncovered evidence that Cabot actually did set sail in a westward direction as soon as possible after receiving the king's permission.

Vigneras found a letter among centuries-old records, written by English merchant John Day to the almirante mayor (grand admiral) of Castile, Spain. Day gives his reader information relating to Cabot's first failed attempt to cross the Atlantic Ocean. "He [Cabot] went with one ship, his crew confused him, he was short of supplies and ran into bad weather and he decided to turn back," read the letter, according to James A. Williamson's book, *The Cabot Voyages*. Since the discovery of that letter, historians have concluded that Day was writing to Columbus.

Historians have long puzzled over Cabot's reason for waiting more than a year to set sail from England. The Day letter says that Cabot took advantage of the king's support immediately. That failed effort may have been the result of a distrustful crew who feared the cold ocean waters. Perhaps doubting his acclaimed expertise, Cabot's men may have been frightened by dangerous ocean storms and revolted against their captain. They likely refused to take the ship in the direction Cabot commanded. With no other choice, the explorer returned to Bristol to wait for better weather conditions and more supplies.

More Preparations

No one knows about the specific plans Cabot made for his voyages. The charter of 1496 from King Henry VII granted the explorer permission to take "five ships or vessels of whatsoever burden and quality they may be, and with so many and with such mariners and men as they may wish to take with them," according to Williamson in *The Cabot Voyages*. In that same letter, however, the king promised no money from the royal exchequer

This painting depicts the departure of John and Sebastian Cabot from Bristol on the elder Cabot's first voyage. Although both John Cabot and his son Sebastian are often illustrated as sailing together, historians have never been able to verify that the two men ever traveled on the same ship or voyage.

(England's department of revenue). He placed all of the responsibility for financing the ship on Cabot, who sought the aid of area merchants.

If Cabot planned his voyage as a hired expert for Bristol's merchants in order to locate the lost island of Brasil, then as the poor man he was known to be, Cabot must have relied on other benefactors to pay for his journey.

Although Henry VII had approved sending five ships in his name, only one small ship set sail from Bristol in May 1497. A *navicula* (little ship) capable of carrying a mere fifty tons of wine and needing a crew of no more than twenty to maneuver and maintain her, was all Cabot had at his disposal for this journey.

The Famous Voyage

Cabot set sail from Bristol, England, in late May 1497, most likely May 22. He would have sailed early in the morning to catch the outgoing tides that carried his ship down the River Avon and into the Bristol Channel.

Cabot set forth aboard the *Matthew* (also spelled *Mathew*, a ship certainly named after Cabot's wife, Mattea), a small, three-masted vessel, with a crew of eighteen to twenty men. He was excited and nervous at the adventure ahead, knowing that the ocean winds could propel him westward or force him once again back to England.

Cabot's ship, the *Matthew*, is seen leaving Bristol in this image. In 1997, a replica of the *Matthew* followed the same course as Cabot in 1497 and sailed across the Atlantic Ocean to Newfoundland. It carried the same number of crew members as the original and took the same amount of time to complete the crossing. Today, the replica of the *Matthew* sits in Bristol harbor. Tourists can board it and take trips around the area.

The most detailed account of Cabot's voyage survives in a letter written by John Day, the same sailor who wrote to Columbus about Cabot's first failed voyage. Day wrote to an Italian explorer who had also made two crossings of the Atlantic. His experience enabled him to include nautical facts that have given historians detailed accounts of Cabot's journey, based on conversations with the explorer himself.

From the Bristol Channel, Cabot set his course for Dursey Head, Ireland, a promontory (highest point) of the island's south-western tip. Once there, Cabot dropped anchor and made evening sightings of the North Star before the main journey began. Cabot intended to follow the line of latitude that crosses Dursey Head in a northerly direction. With his bearings taken, he commanded his crew to weigh anchor, and his journey into unknown waters began.

His voyage took up to thirty-three days, according to Day. An east-northeast wind and calm seas made for a fast journey. It is likely, however, that Cabot spent some of this time struggling against variable winds and skirting ice floes still floating in the cold spring waters.

Rear admiral and historian, Samuel Eliot Morison (1887–1976), who served in the U.S. Naval Reserve during World War II, captured the sense of Cabot's voyage in his book, *The European Discovery of North America*. In his research, Morison crossed the Atlantic Ocean along Cabot's route and studied the documents and maps of the fifteenth and sixteen centuries. Morison's image of Cabot shows a man tacking (adjusting the sails to change direction) across winds that did not blow due east. Cabot likely would have needed to sail around icebergs in western waters. Fog often shrouds the coast north of central Nova Scotia (45° latitude), and Cabot would have needed to use his navigational skills to find his way through that fog.

Possible Landfalls

No one knows exactly where John Cabot landed on June 24, 1497. Since the late 1700s, historians have speculated that Cabot set foot as far north as Baffin Island or as far south as Cape Cod, Massachusetts. Below are some of the most widely believed locations of Cabot's official landing site, listed from north to south.

In Canada

Baffin Island
Cape Chidley, northern tip of Labrador
Near Domino, south of Sandwich Bay, Labrador
Cape St. Lewis, near Fox Harbour, Labrador
Cape Bonavista, Newfoundland
Cape Dégrat, Newfoundland
Cape Race, Newfoundland
Cape Bauld, Newfoundland, in the Strait of Belle Isle
Cape North, island of Cape Breton, Nova Scotia
Cape Sable, southwest Nova Scotia

In the United States

Maine
Cape Cod, Massachusetts

Near the journey's end, Cabot would have sensed land looming ahead. He would have seen low-lying clouds and pieces of trees and plants drifting on the water, and even smelled the aromas of fir trees as they wafted out from the shore. At that, he would have begun taking soundings, which involves dropping the lead weight into the sea to check its depth. He also would have brought up samples from the ocean floor. Early one June morning, at 5:00 AM, according to a map drawn years later by Cabot's son Sebastian, a rugged shore rose before the *Matthew*, as a breeze dispersed the early morning fog.

On June 24, 1497, Cabot, a Genoa-born, Venetian navigator with a small crew of sailors from southern England, set foot upon the shores of North America and officially claimed its land for England.

A Historic Landfall

That long day, a few days after the summer began, became memorable for Cabot and his son Sebastian, who recalled it almost fifty years later. It also marked the date of the feast of St. John the Baptist, the day that celebrates the birth of this New Testament prophet.

The location of Cabot's landfall, however, remains puzzling. The shore, after all, was unknown to all who sailed on the

Cabot would have encountered a scene like this upon his landing in what is now Newfoundland. This is the rocky coastline of Hudson Bay near Fort Prince of Wales, in Churchill, Manitoba, Canada.

Matthew. With no surviving ship logs to record Cabot's navigational readings from his cross-staff, astrolabe, or compass, historians find themselves having to piece together bits of information from letters and copies of maps drawn in the 1500s.

Morison believed that Cabot landed in Griquet Harbor, four miles south of Cape Dégrat, which on modern maps would be on the top of Cape Bauld on the northern-most shore of Newfoundland. Other historians are less certain.

57

This image shows Cabot landing at Labrador, which is thought to be the first part of the New World explored by Europeans. Archaeological evidence has shown that Norse voyagers reached Newfoundland and Labrador around AD 1000.

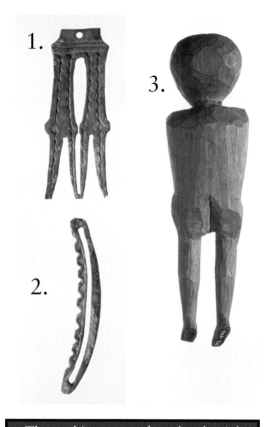

1.

3.

2.

These objects were found at burial sites in Notre Dame Bay in Newfoundland, Canada. Items one and two are bone pendants that were attached to burial bags or hung on clothing. The wooden figure was found in the burial site of a small boy.

During the 1800s and 1900s, scholars argued that Cabot's landfall may have taken place as far north as Baffin Island in Canada, or as far south as Cape Cod, Massachusetts.

Cabot and his crew went ashore the morning of first sighting and raised several flags, most likely the coat of arms of King Henry VII. Some sources mention the flag of St. Mark, the emblem of Venice. Others think Cabot raised either a crucifix or a flag to honor Pope Alexander VI, the leader of the Roman Catholic Church from 1491 to 1503.

Once onshore, Cabot and his crew "found tall trees of the kind masts are made, and other smaller trees," Day said in his letters as told in Williamson's *The Cabot Voyages*. They also found a trail that led inland, a site where a campfire had once burned, and a stick some eighteen inches long that had been pierced at both ends, carved, and painted red. Cabot also reported finding snares for capturing animals and needles for making nets, all signs that the lands were inhabited.

The brief exploration of land on that June morning was the only time Cabot or his crew set foot on this "new found land." Not sure of the reception they would receive from the inhabitants, and being on one defenseless ship with a small crew, Cabot chose to be careful. Indeed, thinking he was in Asia, Cabot would have good reason to be cautious. He knew from his travels to the Middle East that the land was well inhabited. He would not have wanted to risk the lives of his crew and fail to return to England with news of his discovery.

After leaving that landfall, Cabot guided the *Matthew* along the coast of eastern Canada, exploring the bays and inlets, mapping his findings, and searching for any signs of inhabitants. The forest was dense and beautiful, and there were what appeared to be small villages dotting the shoreline. The crew found an abundance of fish, as Williamson reported in *The Cabot Voyages*, "like those in Iceland [that] are dried in the open and sold in England and other countries," and that are sometimes called stockfish in England. Cabot and his crew also saw the shadows of two forms running after one another on land but could not determine whether they were human beings or animals.

Many archaeologists and historians suggest that those stockfish, also known as cod, were England's primary reason for seeking out new lands to explore. Fifteenth-century fisheries of western Europe, particularly those near Iceland, had been badly depleted of this main source of food.

Sea of Peril

The few surviving documents that describe Cabot's journey cannot capture the challenge or the danger of that Canadian coastline, according to Morison. These were new waters for Cabot, who was a very intelligent man and experienced navigator. But an expert mariner, Morison argued, would have known the dangers of facing unknown waters and shores.

The coast Cabot sailed is as rugged a shoreline now as it was in the late 1400s. Treacherous rocks hide below murky waters, while icebergs, even in the summer, cause hazards for sailors of the largest ships. Fog rolls offshore unexpectedly and hides the shoreline even at close distances. While thirty days may sound like a short trip, considering the mission to discover a new land and perhaps encounter people, Cabot's primary goal was to return to England with maps of his journey to help himself and sailors like him repeat the trip. He would not have risked his ship or his crew, historians argue, in any more exploration than they would have needed to establish their "discovery" and document it for their English sponsors.

The Voyage Home

In his letters, Day suggested that Cabot returned to his original landing site before setting his return course. The highly experienced mariner wanted to follow the same path home that he had taken on the outward crossing. "They returned to the coast of Europe in fifteen days," Day wrote.

The trouble Cabot experienced on the return voyage did not come from the weather or the ocean, but from his crew. The sailors he had hired in Bristol lacked confidence in his navigational instruments and in his skills. After all, Cabot was using instruments well known in port cities such as Venice, Genoa, and Portugal, but little used in England. "They had the wind behind them, and he reached Brittany because the sailors confused him saying that he was heading too far north," Day continued. The Bristol merchant sailors had hired an expert and then not trusted his expertise. Still, it was common for the opinions of the ship's crew to have influence on its course.

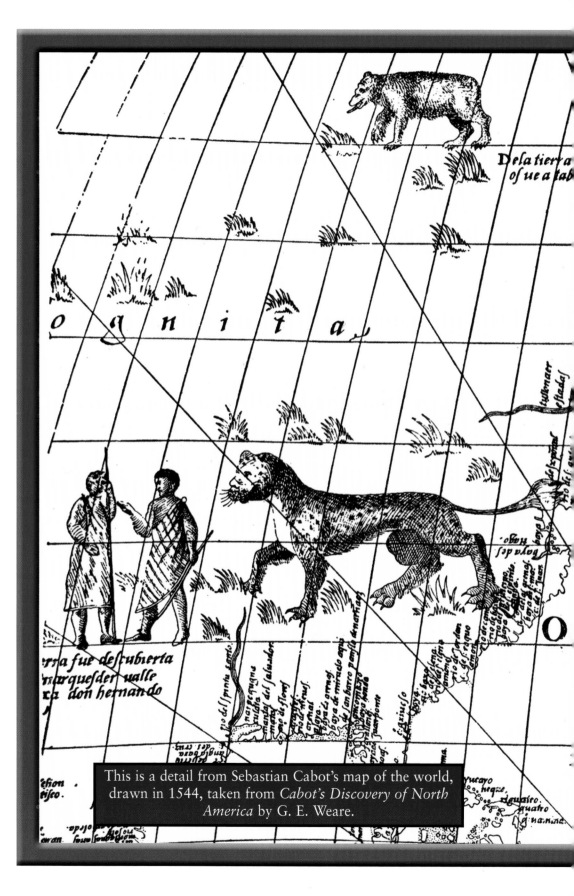

This is a detail from Sebastian Cabot's map of the world, drawn in 1544, taken from *Cabot's Discovery of North America* by G. E. Weare.

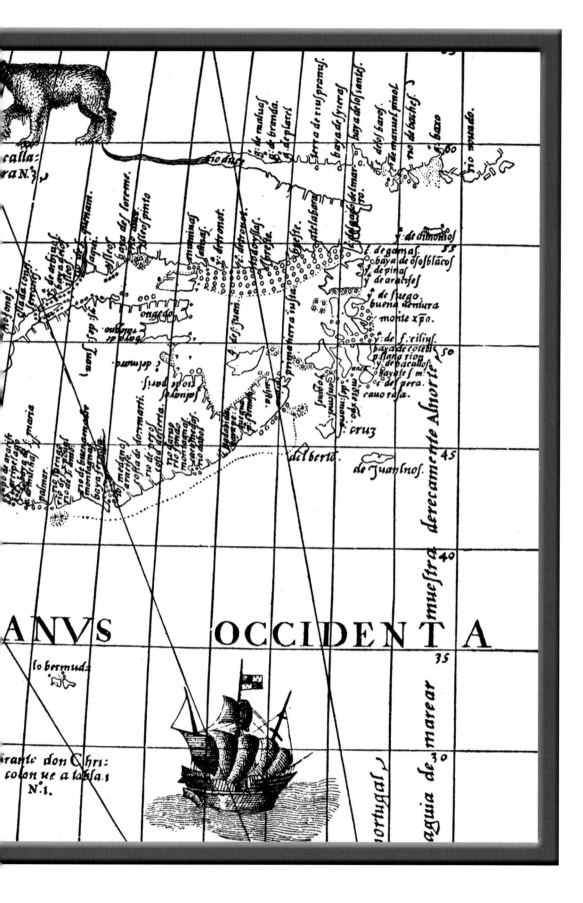

Sent off of his original course by his doubting crew, Cabot drew on his experience to recognize the coast of Brittany in northeastern France. First he tested the ocean bottom, and, recognizing the composition of the sea floor, as well as the lay of the land, Cabot turned north-by-northwest and spent three days sailing familiar waters from France to Bristol. He arrived at his home port on or about August 9, 1497.

5

ONE FINAL VOYAGE

The fleet he prepared, which consisted of five vessels, was pro-
visioned for a year. News has come that one of these, in which
sailed another Friar Buil, has made land in Ireland in a great
storm with the ship badly damaged. The Genoese kept on his way.
—Letter written in 1498 from Pedro de Ayala to the king
and queen of Spain

John Cabot returned safely to England in 1497. He and his crew lived to share the knowledge that they gathered on their nearly three-month-long journey.

Within days of landing in Bristol, Cabot crossed England, a three-day journey by coach, and met with King Henry VII in London. The haste of his travel and the fact that he appeared to have left within a day or two of reaching Bristol's docks suggests that the king was very interested in Cabot's report. That the explorer had successfully planted England's flag on a distant land would bring with it a great claim for Henry VII and all of England.

Records kept of the king's schedule suggest that Henry VII listened to Cabot's report and granted him an immediate gift of ten pounds—a generous sum—as well as an annual pension of twenty pounds.

Cabot's crew had confirmed and supported their commander's story, a fact that made it more believable. In fact, without his English crew to corroborate his findings, Cabot would have had far greater trouble convincing the king that what he said was truthful, according to information attributed to de Soncino in Williamson's *The Cabot Voyages*: "This Messer Zoane [Cabot] as a foreigner and a poor man, would not have obtained credence, had it not been that his companions, who are practically all English and from Bristol, testified that he spoke the truth."

Cabot apparently shared news of the distant land with his many friends, colleagues, and countrymen. Williamson also tells of Cabot's peers who spoke of his now-famous voyage. Lorenzo Pasqualigo, another merchant, wrote on August 23, 1497, "That Venetian of ours who went with a small ship from Bristol to find new islands has come back and says he has discovered mainland 700 leagues away, which is the country of the Grand Khan."

London was a bustling city in the fifteenth century and the political capital of England. The famous Tower of London was built in the eleventh century, and Westminster Abbey was built in the fourteenth century. London was ravaged by the plague in 1665, and much of the city was destroyed in the great fire of 1666. Though devastating, many saw the fire as fortunate, as it eradicated the plague and provided an opportunity to rebuild the city in a more organized manner.

Moreover, Cabot spoke at length with de Soncino, who retold the tale of his voyage to the duke of Milan in a letter written on December 18, 1497. "He [Cabot] tells this in such a way, and makes everything so plain, that I also feel compelled to believe him. What is much more, his Majesty [Henry VII], who is wise and not prodigal, also gives him some credence."

Perhaps, as a way to convince his backers to finance another journey, Cabot created both a flat map and a globe of his voyage. De Ayala, the junior Spanish ambassador to England, mentioned the map in a letter dated July 25, 1498: "I have seen the map made by the discoverer, who is another Genoese like Columbus." Unfortunately, the map and globe are lost to history.

If Cabot left these items in the care of his partners, as some historians have suggested, those partners lost track of them centuries ago. Historical cartographers greatly regret that his illustrations of the journey did not survive. If they had, Cabot's landfall might be as well known as Columbus's. As it is, maps of uncertain quality, copied by people who did not themselves make the journeys they represented, are all that remain to testify to Cabot's voyages. To make matters worse, those maps typically contain confusing dates, latitudes, directions, and perspectives.

No journal that Cabot might have written has survived, if, indeed, he ever wrote any. A captain's log was not yet a part of navigational tradition, and it is possible that Cabot did not keep a personal diary of his journey. However, Renaissance merchants were known to keep nautical charts of their voyages, information they very often saved. In this way, as they traveled the coasts of Europe and Africa they could record latitude, compass settings, and conditions of the ocean's bottom to aid their recollection or to compare to what other sailors had before told them. Still, if Cabot kept such charts, they have also perished.

From poorly copied maps and secondhand written accounts, cartographers have tried to identify the lands Cabot explored. With little more than a general sense of his approximate positions, however, determining the exact route of his voyage has been impossible.

Plans to Return

Enthusiasm for Cabot's official discovery of lands across the Atlantic Ocean was so great that Henry VII, the merchants of Bristol, and Cabot himself began planning a larger expedition for the summer of 1498. Dreams of wealth and fame filled their imaginations.

71

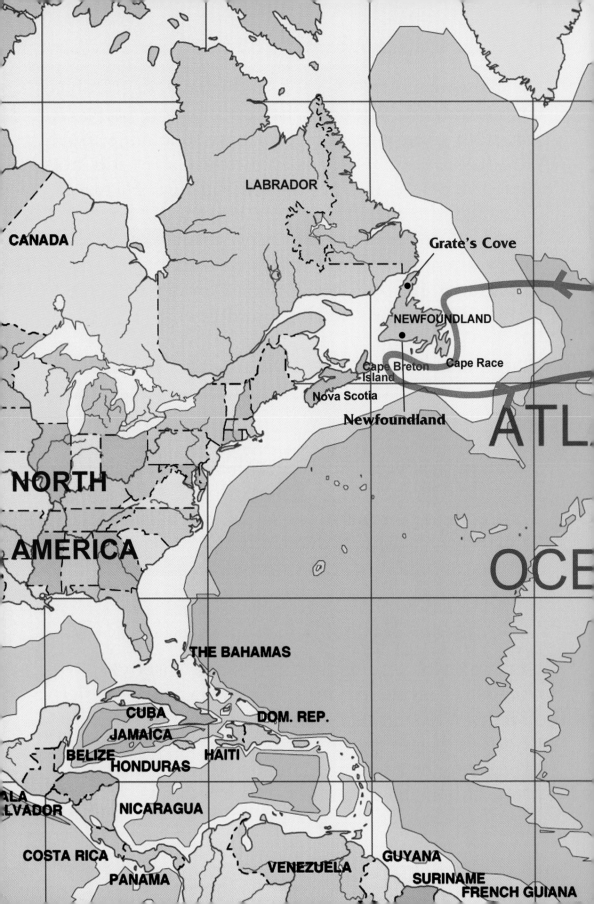

CANADA

LABRADOR

Grate's Cove

NEWFOUNDLAND

Cape Race

Cape Breton
Island

Nova Scotia

Newfoundland

NORTH

AMERICA

ATLA

OCE

THE BAHAMAS

CUBA

JAMAICA

DOM. REP.

BELIZE

HONDURAS

HAITI

ALA
LVADOR

NICARAGUA

COSTA RICA

GUYANA

PANAMA

VENEZUELA

SURINAME

FRENCH GUIANA

Cabot's voyages are shown on this modern map of the world. His 1498 voyage remains mysterious to this day. Historians have speculated that he may have been shipwrecked off the Avalon Peninsula near a place called Grate's Cove in Newfoundland, where he may have swam ashore. If so, Cabot most likely died either of starvation or at the hand of local Indian tribes.

In August 1497, Lorenzo Pasqualigo wrote, "The king has promised him for the spring ten armed ships as he desires and has given him all the prisoners to be sent away, that they may go with him, as he has requested." It was not unusual for criminals to be assigned duties aboard voyages of discovery and exploration, especially because their lives were not as valued as those of typical citizens. In fact, Columbus's crew on his first voyage to the New World was primarily composed of men who were convicted of one crime or another. They sailed with the then-unknown navigator in exchange for their freedom.

The official records of Milan also contain a summary of news received by the duke in letters that arrived the morning of August 24, 1497. The documents briefly reported Cabot's safe return from his journey across the Atlantic Ocean. In the height of excitement over Cabot's news, they also reported, "This next spring his Majesty means to send him with fifteen or twenty ships."

In December 1497, in a lengthy letter to the duke of Milan, de Soncino wrote this about Cabot's plans for 1498: "Messer Zoane . . . proposes to keep along the coast from the place at which he touched, more and more towards the east, until he reaches an island which he calls Cipango, situated in the equinoctial [equator] region, where he believes that all the spices of the world have their origin as well as the jewels."

Day, the Bristol merchant, wrote to his correspondent in late 1497, "With God's help it is hoped to push through plans for exploring the said land more thoroughly next year with ten or twelve vessels," as told in Williamson's book, *The Cabot Voyages.*

The months that followed Cabot's return to England were lavish indeed. He is said to have become rather boastful of his accomplishments, parading around the city of Bristol and making promises of riches and land to all of his new friends. These were the promises of a returning hero, John Cabot, a man who quickly became famous in the streets of London. Crowds followed Cabot. People sought him out, paid attention to his speeches, called him "Admiral," and admired the silks he now wore, signs of the king's favors. His crew acted like noble counts led by Cabot, their glorified prince.

Those were the hopes of a man with proof that his dream had come true; one who believed, like Columbus had, that he had actually found a sea route to the riches of Asia. While Columbus struggled among his islands, he had found the Asian mainland.

On his second journey westward, Cabot was to command more than a dozen ships, fitted with a crew of hundreds, not merely a single ship with a crew of eighteen. On them he would carry enough supplies for more than a year of exploration. On this voyage, Cabot and

Italian explorer John Cabot worked closely with the merchants of Bristol, England, to plan his journey across the Atlantic Ocean. Based on Cabot's first success, these merchants were willing to help finance a larger, second expedition. Cabot never returned from that second voyage, which set sail from Bristol in 1498.

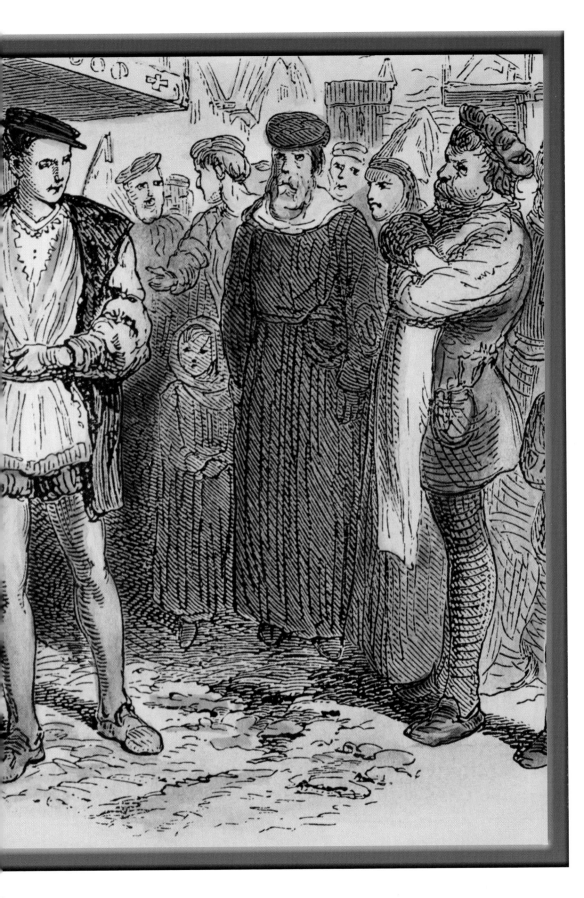

his crew would be prepared to establish an English colony on the claimed shores. They would build a fortress and from there explore the coastline, braving any possible dangers.

After his tremendous and profitable meeting with the king, with promises of a great expedition to plan, Cabot returned to his wife and sons at their rented home in Bristol, near one of the city's main docks. It was there that Cabot made plans for his second expedition.

Funds for England's Admiral

By early 1498, Cabot's great dreams were scaled back when the support for his second voyage was decreased. The king, having fought wars against rebels in his own country, did not have the money to spend on risky ocean ventures. On February 3, 1498, Henry VII issued his second letter patent to Cabot. It described plans for a much smaller second voyage than Cabot had hoped to lead: "By thies presentes geve and graunte to our wel beloved John Kaboto [Cabot], Venician, sufficient auctorite and power that he . . . may take at his pleasure vi [six] englisshe shippes . . . and theym convey and lede [lead] to the londe [land] and Iles [islands] of late founde by the seid [said] John in our name."

Expense accounts from the king's official records show that, although he granted permission for six ships to sail, he would finance only one vessel. The king's decision is seen by some historians as stingy in comparison to investments made by other monarchs. The Spanish monarchs, King Ferdinand and Queen Isabella, made generous contributions to finance Columbus's journeys. And the support given by the Portuguese monarchs John II (1481–1495) and Manuel I (1495–1521) to find a route around the southern tip of Africa, now known as the Cape of Good Hope, was extensive. One explanation is that England's king was indeed a frugal man, eager to give permission but not money. It seemed that he was willing to let the rich merchants take the risk of exploration while he took all the credit. Still another explanation is that in the late 1400s, England was not yet the world power she would later become under the reign of King Henry VIII (1509–1547) and still later under the leadership of Elizabeth I (1558–1603). Without much confidence of bringing England greater claim to Asia, Henry VII made a very small official investment in Cabot's second trip.

Business records from the Bristol archives indicate that merchants financed four additional ships. Although they had viewed Cabot's maps and seen or heard of maps made of Columbus's voyages, Cabot's business partners may not have been convinced by either explorer that the lands they had encountered were, in fact, the shores of Asia. Without greater evidence that the Spice Islands of Asia were within reach, these businessmen, like their king, would not, and perhaps could not, invest any more money in Cabot's voyage. And Cabot, once a poor man, apparently had no riches of his own that he wished to invest in the journey. The yearly pension that Henry VII had granted him in August 1497 was not paid until early 1498. Though it was enough to improve his lifestyle and allow him to live well, it was not the sort of wealth necessary to purchase and outfit a sailing ship. Still, Cabot's five ships were more than Columbus's first three, but less than the fleet of fifteen that he took on his second voyage to the West Indies.

The Second Voyage

With five ships committed to his venture, Cabot put to sea in early May 1498. As recorded in the official *Chronicles of London*, the ships carried with them many goods suitable for trading, such as cloth, lace, and wool.

Cabot chose to follow the same route in 1498 that he had taken in 1497. He sailed from Bristol to the southwestern coast of Ireland and may have followed the 51° north line of latitude westward to Newfoundland. Unfortunately, Cabot's second voyage, however well supplied, was destined for complete failure.

Pedro de Ayala, Spain's junior ambassador to England, wrote to his sovereigns Ferdinand and Isabella in July 1498 that "news has come that one of these, in which sailed another Friar Buil, has made land in Ireland in a great storm with the ship badly damaged. The Genoese [Cabot] kept on his way."

Five ships set sail from Ireland. A great storm hit. One ship turned back, while the others, with Cabot among those on board, continued on. The small fleet was apparently lost at sea. Official records, personal letters, and even history books written in the mid-1500s do not tell the story of what happened to Cabot or to the others on board those four large ships. The admiral's dreams of riches, as well as his dreams of a place in history, ended abruptly.

Cabot's name appears again in England's records, but in a confusing array of locations. Polydore Vergil, an Italian priest who became an English citizen and close friend of King Henry VII, wrote of the explorer's voyages and tragic death in his famous histories of England in 1512–1513, a chronicle that was later published in 1534. The published versions of Vergil's history do not include Cabot's name, but notes on the document, preserved in the Vatican library in Rome, show the name "Ioanne Cabot" inserted in spaces that Vergil had left blank. That suggests to some that as

81

In 1997, actors set sail from Bristol on a replica of the *Matthew* to re-enact John Cabot's voyage to Newfoundland for the film *People of the Sea*. Here, actors Henia Farley *(left)* and Simon Farley hoist the main sail on board the *Matthew* at Weymouth Harbor in Bristol, England.

little as fifteen years after his successful crossing of the Atlantic, people had already forgotten about the explorer.

Cabot apparently died on that 1498 voyage. Like so much about his life, history records nothing certain about his death.

6

THE FUTURE
OF ENGLAND

John set out in this same year [1498] and sailed first to Ireland. Then he set sail towards the west. In the event he is believed to have found the new lands nowhere but on the very bottom of the ocean, to which he is thought to have descended together with his boat, the victim himself of that self-same ocean; since after that voyage he was never seen again anywhere.
— Polydore Vergil, 1512–1513, from the Latin manuscript of *Anglica Historia*

John Cabot's fate remains an unanswered question, like so much of his life story. King Henry VII's day book, an official record of his daily activities, showed the payment of a pension to Cabot after the summer of 1498, but it does not say to whom that payment was made. Historians suggest that Cabot's wife could have received the money in the belief that her husband would return some time in 1499.

This illustration depicts John and Sebastian Cabot as they might have appeared on the deck of the *Matthew*, though historians speculate whether or not Sebastian ever sailed with his father. This artist's depiction shows the Cabots as they may have appeared leaving Labrador, off the coast of Newfoundland, to make their way back to England.

Rent on Cabot's home in Bristol was also received sometime in late 1498, but again, no one knows precisely who paid that bill.

Cabot may have once again reached the shores of Newfoundland. Only one ship returned to Ireland after encountering the rough storm. The other four may have continued onward. In 1501, the Venetian ambassador in Portugal wrote a letter to his brother in Venice. According to James Williamson in *The Cabot Voyages*, the letter described the homecoming of Gaspar Corte Real, a Portuguese explorer who sailed the eastern coast of the North American continent in 1500. "These men have brought from there a piece of broken gilt sword, which certainly seems to have been made in Italy. One of the boys was wearing in his ears two silver rings which without doubt seem to have been made in Venice," the letter stated.

These artifacts have suggested to some historians that Cabot, or at least members of his 1498 expedition, did actually reach the shores of Newfoundland. Other historians argue that any sailors traveling from any European port to the New World could have left those artifacts behind, including Cabot during his first voyage.

No one served as a spokesperson for Cabot to tell of his explorations, as did Ferdinand Columbus, son of Christopher, who wrote a biography of his father. In many ways, uncontrollable fates effectively prevented generations of people who looked back on Cabot's accomplishments from seeing clearly, or faintly, his contribution to Europe's influence over North and South America.

England's Future

With such little historical evidence regarding Cabot, scholars have proposed theories about hidden events that may explain the uneven historical record that does survive.

James Williamson suggests that soon after Cabot's voyage of 1498, perhaps even as a result of it, England's royalty and members of its wealthy upper class underwent a change of thought regarding the "new found land" that Cabot had explored. Official documents in the king's records, including letters, record books, and preserved discussions of the westward adventures of explorers and merchants, no longer refered to Cipango, Cathay, or the dream of reaching Asia by a shorter ocean route. Still, even if England knew that Cabot had not reached Asia, the explorer may have died without realizing this himself.

Cabot's dream of a westerly ocean voyage to Asia seemed to fade from discussion, replaced by the realization that a continent lay between England and Asia. Less

King Henry VII and John Cabot are shown in this fifteenth-century painting. Although Cabot's explorations seemed fruitless at the time, they helped England establish a foothold in North America.

than ten years after Cabot's successful voyage, records refer to a "new found land" as a continent and a barrier in their efforts to reach Asia. By the very early 1500s, explorers, including Cabot's son Sebastian, had begun seeking a Northwest Passage through this new land to those Asian riches.

Though his dream did not come true, Cabot's voyage of 1497 was an important event in England's history. With his stories, maps, globes, and the testimony of his crew, he revealed the existence of a land no more than 2,000 miles to the west.

It took more than a century for Cabot's discovery to become significant to England's efforts to colonize the New World. Though explorations continued, it was not until 1607 that England established Jamestown, its first official settlement in the New World, except for the failed Roanoke colony, in what would later become the state of Virginia.

Historians suggest that the most valuable contribution of Cabot's journey was that it gave England a basis to stake a claim to the lands in the New World. King Henry VII and his son, Henry VIII, did not act aggressively upon the potential of that new land, but without the king's participation in the venture, England would have been weakened in its competition with Spain, Portugal, and France in laying any claim to new lands on distant shores.

Sebastian Cabot, who followed in his father's footsteps as an explorer, took advantage of his father's death and subsequent fall into obscurity. Sebastian falsely claimed that he had led the two voyages to the New World, not John Cabot, thus securing for himself a place in history while his father was practically forgotten.

Conflicts in Europe between England and its rivals slowed efforts of exploration, but Cabot's voyage paved the way for a century of discovery of the shores of Labrador, Newfoundland, Nova Scotia, and Maine. Indeed, Sebastian Cabot is credited by some historians with having explored Hudson Bay in Canada in 1509, almost 100 years before English navigator Henry Hudson, for whom it is named, did so.

Cabot's successful voyage had proved to England that tremendously rich fishing waters lay less than a month's journey across the Atlantic Ocean. Twentieth-century archaeologists and historians have suggested that these waters, with their ample supplies of cod, motivated Bristol's merchants to continue financing fishing fleets to harvest the fish for the wealth it brought.

The Mystery Remains

Five hundred years after his voyage to the New World, John Cabot remains an intriguing mystery. Some people, in fact, claim that Cabot is one of history's greatest forgotten heroes.

Writers have hailed Cabot as the man who contributed more to the wealth of England than any other explorer. He returned to England from one brief journey with knowledge of a land that lay just a short voyage across the ocean to the west. In the name of one small island nation, England, Cabot laid claim to a vast continent.

King Henry VII may have been disappointed that his discovery was not in fact Asia. Over the course of history, however, Cabot's voyages and the flags he planted on behalf of England gave that country the beginning it needed to build a stronger kingdom.

Today, colleges in Canada are named after Cabot. The people of Newfoundland, Nova Scotia, and English-speaking Canada view this Venetian merchant as the true

This plaque commemorating the life and voyages of John Cabot is set in a stone at the Cabot Beach Provincial Park, near Malpeque, on Prince Edward Island, Canada.

European "discoverer" of North America. Though Cabot has never been commemorated in Canada as Columbus has been in the United States, the Canadians take pride in the one voyage of this sailor who gave to England the clear directions to a new world of riches.

In the late 1800s, the English port city of Bristol built a monument to Cabot, a 150-foot tower that stands on Brandon Hill and overlooks the city. In 1997, Cabot enthusiasts set sail across the Atlantic Ocean in a re-creation of the *Matthew*'s journey. They followed Cabot's presumed route to Newfoundland, maintained life on board as Cabot and his crew would have done, and took just as many days to reach the mainland. A replica of the *Matthew* now resides at Bristol's docks. Guests may venture aboard the ship and even join the crew as they take her on short ocean tours.

Cabot's journey has been hard to re-create. Anyone concerned with retelling it accurately must struggle with a scarce supply of original documents and too little information. None have been able to bring Cabot's story into clear focus. In fact, even visual artists over the centuries have had to turn to their own imaginations to paint and sculpt portraits of the explorer, since no images of him have survived.

The work of discovering Cabot is not finished. Documents continue to surface in the twentieth-first century, so historians have some hope that detailed research will at last reveal to the world a precise story of Cabot's contributions during the great age of exploration.

CHRONOLOGY

1000 Approximate date that Leif Eriksson sails to North America.

1298 Marco Polo writes about his travels to Asia, exciting Europeans about the riches there.

1450 Probable year of birth of John Cabot.

1453 Constantinople falls to the Turks and sparks interest in new trade routes to the East.

1480s English merchant ships sail throughout the waters of the Atlantic Ocean, possibly as far west as North America.

1492 Christopher Columbus sails to the New World, a land he believes is near Asia's shoreline.

1494 The Treaty of Tordesillas divides western discoveries between Spain and Portugal with an imaginary line from the North Pole to the South Pole.

1497 Cabot sails to Newfoundland, Canada, under England's flag.

1498 Vasco da Gama finds a new trade route to India by sailing around the coast of Africa. Cabot is lost at sea and presumed dead.

1499 Amerigo Vespucci explores the South American coastline.

1507 Sebastian Cabot sails to North America. The first map is printed naming North and South America after Vespucci.

1519–1522 Ferdinand Magellan circumnavigates Earth.

1607 Jamestown, the first permanent settlement of the English in the New World, is founded.

GLOSSARY

astrolabe A navigator's tool used to determine latitude. It is a small, circular device, with four spokes reaching from the outer ring to a central hub and meeting at right angles in its center.

Brasil The Isle of Brasil, a legendary island far to the west of England in the Atlantic Ocean. Also, a term often found on European maps made before 1500 to designate unknown islands in the distant Atlantic Ocean.

cartographer A person who works with or makes maps and/or charts.

Cathay An old European name for China, often used during the Middle Ages and the Renaissance.

Cipango   A mysterious island of medieval European legend, believed to lie east of Asia, but generally identified in modern times as Japan.

city-state   An independent city that is itself a separate nation. Venice and Genoa were powerful city-states during the Middle Ages and the Renaissance.

cross-staff   An instrument for measuring the angle of elevation of heavenly bodies. It was made of a long rod, or staff, calibrated in degrees with a shorter second rod, perpendicular to the first, that slid up and down the long rod. It was used to measure latitude by determining the position of the North Star.

dominion   A territory that is governed; having absolute ownership over something.

dowry   The property given to a husband from his wife's family.

elude   To remain hidden or unknown; to escape detection.

exchequer   Under the English government system, the department responsible for the country's revenue.

Genoa   A present-day city in northwestern Italy on the Ligurian Sea; in the 1500s, a powerful city-state and leading commercial center.

league   In navigational terms, a unit of measure equaling about three miles in English-speaking countries. However, the length of a league has varied over time and across nations, making the determination of the exact distance difficult.

Milan   A powerful city and seat of the duchy (a region ruled by a duke) of Milan, in northern Italy.

monarch   The hereditary ruler of a nation that follows a governmental structure; a king or queen.

patent letter   A public or open letter granting rights or privileges to someone; an official document or contract.

patronage   The support and encouragement of a wealthy sponsor, often given in the form of money, to a person with talent and skills who does not have the wealth to be self-supporting.

quadrant   A navigational instrument used for measuring latitude, consisting of a quarter circle, marked in degrees, and a moveable rod for aligning with the North Star.

sanction   To give official approval to or for; to authorize.

Simancas   A city of ancient origins in north central Spain.

Venice   A modern city in northeastern Italy on the Adriatic Sea; in the 1500s, it was an extensive city-state, governing much of the surrounding lands.

FOR MORE INFORMATION

The Mariners' Museum
100 Museum Drive
Newport News, VA 23606
(757) 596-2222
Web site: http://www.mariner.org

The National Maritime Museum
Greenwich, London
SE10 9NF
England
(+44) 208 858 4422
Web site: http://www.nmm.ac.uk

Web Sites

Due to the changing nature of Internet links, the Rosen
Publishing Group, Inc., has developed an online list of Web
sites related to the subject of this book. This site is updated
regularly. Please use this link to access the list:
http://www.rosenlinks.com/lee/joca/

FOR FURTHER READING

Brown, Warren. *The Search for the Northwest Passage* (World Explorers). Broomall, PA: Chelsea House, 2000.

Chrisp, Peter. *Voyages to the New World*. New York: Thompson Learning, 1993.

Fritz, Jean. *Around the World in a Hundred Years: From Henry the Navigator to Magellan*. New York: Paper Star, 1998.

Lomask, Milton. *Great Lives: Exploration*. New York: Atheneum Books for Young Readers, 1988.

Marcovitz, Hal. *Marco Polo and the Wonders of the East* (Explorers of the New World). Broomall, PA: Chelsea House, 2000.

Matthews, Rupert. *Eyewitness: Explorer* (Eyewitness Books). New York: DK Publishing, 2000.

Shields, Charles J. *John Cabot and the Rediscovery of North America* (Explorers of the New World). Broomall, PA: Chelsea House, 2001.

BIBLIOGRAPHY

Andrews, K. R., N. P. Canny, and P. E. H. Hair, eds. *The Westward Enterprise: English Activities in Ireland, the Atlantic, and America 1480–1650.* Detroit, MI: Wayne State University Press, 1979.

Beazley, Raymond. *John and Sebastian Cabot: The Discovery of North America.* New York: Burt Franklin, 1964.

Biddle, Richard. *A Memoir of Sebastian Cabot: With a Review.* Freeport, NY: Books for Libraries Press, 1970.

Biggar, H. P., ed. *The Precursors of Jacques Cartier 1497–1534: A Collection of Documents Relating to the Early History of the Dominion of Canada.* Ottawa: Government Printing Bureau, 1911.

Bourne, Edward Gaylord, ed. *Original Narratives of Early American History: The Northmen Columbus and Cabot: 985–1503*. New York: Charles Scribner & Sons, 1906.

Cabot Bibliography: With an Introductory Essay on the Careers of the Cabots Based Upon an Independent Examination of the Sources of Information. Bibliographical and Reference Series 99. American Classics in History and Social Science 14. 1900. New York: Burt Franklin, 1967.

Day, John. "John Day to the Lord Grand Admiral." Translated by L. A. Vigneras. Williamson pp. 211–214.

Hakluyt, Richard. *Divers Voyages Touching the Discoverie of America*. Ann Arbor, MI: University Microfilms-Xerox, 1966.

Henry VII. *"First Letters Patent granted by Henry VII to John Cabot and his Sons."* Translated by H. P. Biggar.

Henry VII. *"Second Letters Patent to John Cabot."* Translated by H. P. Biggar.

Hind, Allen B., ed. *Calendar of State Papers and Manuscripts Existing in the Archives and Collections of Milan, Vol. 1*. London: His Majesty's Stationary Office, 1912.

Johnson, Adrian. *America Explored: A Cartographical History of the Exploration of North America.* New York: Viking Press, 1974.

Morison, Samuel Eliot. *The Great Explorers: The European Discovery of America.* New York: Oxford University Press, 1978.

Pope, Peter E. *The Many Landfalls of John Cabot.* Toronto: Univeristy of Toronto Press, 1997.

Porter, Edward G. "The Cabot Celebrations of 1897." *The New England Magazine.* February 1898, pp. 653–671.

Pringle, Heather. "Cabot, Cod and the Colonists: John Cabot's Discoveries and the Influence of Cod Fishery on the Lives of English Colonists in Newfoundland." *Canadian Geographic,* 1997, pp. 30–39.

Quinn, David Beers. *England and the Discovery of America, 1481–1620: From The Bristol Voyages of the Fifteenth Century to the Pilgrim Settlement at Plymouth: The Exploration, Exploitation, and Trial-and Error Colonization of North America by the English.* New York: Alfred A. Knopf, 1973.

Seaver, Kirsten. *The Frozen Echo: Greenland and the Exploration of North America, ca. AD 1000–1500.* Stanford, CA: Stanford University Press, 1996.

Vigneras, L. A. "New Light on the 1497 Cabot Voyage in America." *Hispanic American Historical* Review, 1956, pp. 503–506.

Williamson, James A. *The Cabot Voyages and Bristol Discovery Under Henry VII*. Works Issued by the Hakluyt Society, Second Series 120. Cambridge, England: Hakluyt Society, 1962.

INDEX

About the Author

Marian Rengel is a wife and mother living in central Minnesota. She has worked as a journalist and teacher, and has written many documents and publications, both fiction and nonfiction. This is her first book for young adults.

Photo Credits

Cover, pp. 10, 33, 88 © Archivo Iconografico, S.A./Corbis; p. 4 © Dave G. Houser/Corbis; pp. 13, 64–65 © North Wind Picture Archives; pp. 16–17 © Maps.com/Corbis; pp. 19, 60, 76–77 © Granger Collection; pp. 22, 26–27, 35, 45, 48, 50–51 © Bettmann/Corbis; pp. 30, 68 © Culver Pictures; p. 32 © National Maritime Museum, London; p. 37 © Hulton/Archive/Getty Images; p. 38 General Research Division, The New York Public Library, Astor, Lenox, and Tilden Foundations; pp. 43, 58–59, 90 © SuperStock; p. 53 © Mary Evans Picture Library; p. 57 © Lowell Georgia/Corbis; p. 82 © Cordaiy Photo Library Ltd./Corbis; p. 85 © Stock Montage; pp. 92–93 © James Marshall/Corbis.

Series Design

Tahara Hasan

Layout

Les Kanturek

Editor

Joann Jovinelly